Reptile and A
Keeper's Guides

CRESTED GECKOS AND RELATIVES

R. D. Bartlett

BARRON'S

Acknowledgments

When you begin talking to other reptile fanciers about geckos, you'll realize that they quickly divide themselves into two camps—those who think geckos are interesting and those who are hopelessly, totally entranced by these intriguing lizards. Although not all of the people listed here are inveterate geckophiles, they have all provided me with advice or photographic opportunities. I greatly appreciate and acknowledge the assistance of Ralph Curtis, Mike Ellard, Scott Hearsey, Chuck Hurt, Rob MacInnes (*www.gherp.com*), Sean McKeown, Regis Opferman, Mike Stuhlman, and Tim Tytle.

Special thanks must be given to Bill and Marcia Brant of the Gourmet Rodent (*www.grmtrodent.com*). From the company name, you would initially think only of food animals. After delving a little deeper, you find one of the nation's most professional breeding programs for many species of reptiles, crested geckos among them.

My appreciation is also extended to Brad Teague of "Geckos by Brad" (*www.GeckosbyBrad.com*), who took the time to explain to me some of the terms now used to describe the many colors and patterns of crested geckos now being produced.

All inquiries should be addressed to:
Barron's Educational Series, Inc.
250 Wireless Boulevard
Hauppauge, NY 11788
http://www.barronseduc.com

International Standard Book No. 0-7641-3001-3

Library of Congress Catalog Card No. 2004046138

Library of Congress Cataloging-in-Publication Data
Bartlett, Richard D., 1938–
    Crested geckos and relatives : facts & advice on care
and breeding / R.D. Bartlett.
        p.   cm. — (Reptile/amphibian keeper's guides)
    Includes index.
    ISBN 0-7641-3001-3
        1. Crested geckos as pets. 2. Rhacodactylus. I. Title.
SF459.G35B359   2004
639.3'952—dc22   2004046138

Printed in China
9 8 7 6 5 4 3 2 1

Contents

Introduction

Not until the turn of the twenty-first century did crested geckos become available to most casual North American hobbyists. Prior to that date, choices for a gecko pet had been between the more traditional species—the tokay, the leopard, the fat-tailed, and the more common day geckos, among them. By the year 2000, crested geckos had come into their own. Pet store owners and hobbyists alike found that unlike most tokay geckos, crested geckos did not try to amputate a keeper's finger each time they were handled. Unlike most day geckos, crested geckos were not nervous. They were almost handleable—they did not dart from their tank and scuttle up a wall before they could be retrieved. Unlike the leopard and fat-tailed geckos that liked to remain in a hide box during the hours of daylight, although crested geckos were usually quietly sleeping, they were at least visible as they curled up on a horizontal branch.

Although they were not very colorful, crested geckos *were* different—*very* different—in appearance. These geckos had an immensely broad head, and they really *did* have crests, twin crests in fact. The crests were comprised of two rows of elongate scales. One crest began above each eye (where the scales were longest), continued along the head and body, and ended above the hind legs. No other gecko available in the pet market had such an interesting suite of characters.

Because of herpetocultural success, what had been a $1,500 lizard available to only a few dedicated enthusiasts in 1995 had, by the year 2000, become a $150 lizard that was readily available. As crested geckos truly caught on with hobbyists, the little lizards were incorporated into more and more breeding programs. Today (2004), crested geckos are often available for $50 or less.

A view of a crested gecko's crest.

New Caledonian Geckos

Crested geckos are one of six species in the New Caledonian genus *Rhacodactylus*. Collectively, the geckos of this genus are referred to as giant geckos. If when the word *giant* is spoken you think of a lizard the size of a green iguana or savanna monitor, you may be disappointed by what is a giant among geckos. The largest extant gecko, which *is*, by the way, a member of this New Caledonian genus, only rarely exceeds 1 foot (30 cm) in length. The New Caledonian giant gecko has a record size of only 14.56 inches (36.98 cm). However, when you compare its hefty bulk and foot-long (30 cm) length with the slender 2-inch (50 cm) total length of a reef gecko, the New Caledonian species becomes a true giant. In fact, as far as we know, this giant of geckodom was surpassed in size by only one New Zealand species that is now thought to be extinct. What constitutes a giant is all a matter of perspective.

The second largest of the *Rhacodactylus*, *R. trachyrhynchus*, is a giant of sorts. Commonly referred to as the rough-snouted giant gecko, it attains a length of about 1 foot (30 cm). However, it has a proportionately longer tail and less body bulk than the former species. So when the two are compared, *R. trachyrhynchus* looks by far the smaller of the two species.

Decades ago, Sean McKeown introduced me to the two largest species of giant gecko. Both were then under the care of Sean and his staff at the Chaffee Zoological Gardens in Fresno, California. The size, unique appearance, and quiet demeanor of those gigantic geckos captivated me.

A female crested gecko hides behind a limb.

The rough-snouted giant gecko bears live young.

How about the others, the crested gecko relatives, you ask? Are they available? The answer is yes for at least four of the five remaining species. However, all of those four have proven a little more difficult than the crested gecko to breed, and prices have remained high (see pages 11–13). The remaining species, *R. trachyrhynchus*, is occasionally available in Europe but is almost unknown in America.

Body Form and Behaviors

All giant geckos have expanded toe pads that enable them to climb vertically on smooth surfaces, glass included. Their lidless eyes have elliptical pupils. Their prehensile tails have broadened, flattened tips bearing lamellae, similar in action to those beneath the toes. Giant geckos are omnivorous, consuming insects and fruits and probably lapping nectar, saps, and juices as well. All of the six species are considered to be of vulnerable status.

Territoriality
Sexually mature male giant geckos are extremely territorial and will skirmish constantly with others of their sex to establish territorial dominance. There should never be more than one male kept to a cage. The females, although hierarchical, can usually be kept together. Several juvenile giant geckos can be raised in the same enclosure. However, as the lizards reach sexual maturity, hierarchies are developed

Following that meeting, years passed before I saw any additional species in that genus, and that example just happened to be a crested gecko. I can remember looking at that lizard and saying something to the effect of "Oh my, what a delightful creature."

Gecko-Keeping History

Before it was refound in New Caledonia in 1994, the crested gecko had been thought to be extinct. After its rediscovery, a few were collected. Of these, some were acquired by zoos. The remainder ended up in the private collections of dedicated and talented herpetoculturists. It was these first-available crested geckos that commanded the price of $1,500 each.

Fortunately, the crested gecko proved rather easily bred and today, barely more than 10 years since the lizard's rediscovery, babies of *Rhacodactylus ciliatus* can be purchased in pet stores and from specialty dealers and breeders across much of the world.

This crested gecko is preparing to jump.

and aggressive behavior may be manifested. If kept communally, watch all carefully and be ready to intervene if necessary.

Reproduction

Of the six species of giant geckos, five are oviparous. A healthy female will lay several clutches of two soft-shelled eggs each at monthly intervals throughout the warm months of the year. The sixth species, the rough-snouted giant gecko, *R. trachyrhynchus*, produces either one or two live babies once a year.

In this book, we will primarily discuss the crested gecko, *R. ciliatus*, but much that is said here applies equally to the other species of this genus. Despite having had much success with all members of this genus we, as herpetoculturists, have much yet to learn. This is especially so of the largest species and most so with the live-bearing *R. trachyrhynchus*.

If you maintain any geckos of this genus, please keep records and share your findings with others.

What Are the Giant Geckos?

The crested gecko and its relatives are primarily forest species and are nocturnal. Although small in number, the genus contains not only the largest extant gecko species (the New Caledonian giant gecko), but one additional large species, the rough-snouted giant gecko. The giant gecko may attain a length of a very robust 13.5 inches (34 cm). Of this, only about 4 inches (10 cm) is tail length. The next smaller, the rough-snouted giant gecko, is differently proportioned than its

Crested geckos with dark spots are referred to as the Dalmatian phase.

A Quick Look at a Giant Gecko's Toe and Tail Tip

Most typical geckos have distended toe pads, which allow them to climb even smooth surfaces agilely. The toe pads are more complex than they might seem. They are not adhesive, per se. The pads are transversely divided into a series of lamellae that contain vast numbers of tiny, bristle-like keratinized setae. The setae are tipped with an equally vast number of microscopic, nonskid spatulas with rounded ends. The spatulas and the smooth surface on which the gecko is climbing form weak attractive forces. To appreciate the complexity of these climbing devices fully, simply watch the way a slowly moving gecko curls its toes upward when disengaging a foot. The giant geckos add tail tip lamellae to this security blanket, providing them with a fifth nonskid point of contact while climbing.

The tail tip of all giant geckos is bluntly rounded and bears setae to help the lizards retain their hold.

larger relative. The rough-snouted giant gecko may attain an overall length of about 12 inches (30 cm), but its tail is about 6 inches (15 cm) long. It is of moderate body build. The remaining four species are smaller (7 to 9 inches [18 to 23 cm]), of moderately robust build, and have normally proportioned tails. Interestingly, the tail tip of the geckos of this genus is flattened and rounded, and it bears lamellae on the underside. These transverse scansors contain microcilia that assist a climbing gecko in retaining its grip.

The face of a crested gecko.

What Is the Crested Gecko?

The crested gecko is known scientifically as *Rhacodactylus ciliatus*. This giant gecko attains an adult length of 7 inches (18 cm). Hatchlings are just under 3 inches (7.5 cm) in total length. It is one of the smallest species in the genus, and the only one of the six to have been bred by herpetoculturists in sufficient numbers to have become available to casual hobbyists. It is also the only one of the genus to have a price tag regularly under $100 each.

Why a Favorite?

Unlike many other geckos that have become hobbyist favorites because of a brilliant color, crested geckos seem to have initially gained favor for their perceived rarity. Then they became truly popular when captive-breeding programs showed them to be hardy and interesting captives and were successfully bred enough to allow the prices to drop to a level that could be afforded by casual hobbyists.

Appearance
Crested geckos, in fact all species in this genus, are clad in the dull orange, dull yellow, brown, and gray hues of lichen-encrusted bark rather than the greens of leaves. Some may bear light stripes, others do not. The back is often of a different color (it may be darker or lighter) than the sides, and white patches or stripes occur on the upper surface of the tail.

Color Changing
A certain degree of metachrosis (color changing) is possible. However, this is often merely a darker (nighttime coloration) to a lighter (daytime coloration) ground color. Also, stressed or cold adult examples tend to be darker than when the lizards are content and warm.

This is a large male yellow-phase crested gecko.

This crested gecko is unusual in that it has no contrasting colors.

Red on brown creates a beautiful crested gecko.

The Colors of Crested Geckos

As you can see, crested geckos vary naturally in color. Herpetoculturists are currently striving to highlight certain natural features of crested geckos and to enhance others. Line breeding is developing redder reds and yellower yellows, but no spectacularly different colors have yet been developed.

When you see ads for a crested gecko having colors such as flame orange, flame yellow, orange fire, pastel fire, pinstripe, tiger, Dalmatian, tan, chocolate, and harlequin, what do these terms actually mean? Well, at this writing, there is no standard meaning to most of these terms. What is advertised as a harlequin by one breeder is the flame morph of another. Additionally, the oranges, yellows, and greens are just the brightest examples of a crested gecko's natural coloration. The term *pinstripe* refers to a contrasting color (either lighter or darker) that separates the dorsal color from the lateral color. Dalmatian crested geckos have a variable number of dark spots scattered over their dorsal and lateral surfaces.

What Color Is It Really?

Can a crested gecko be furry? Absolutely not, but those advertised as "furs" bear a profusion of elongate spiny scales over much of their light-to-chocolate body color. The term *beaded* refers to the fact that the scales of the

This crested gecko has lost its tail.

dorsolateral crests are short and tubercle-like rather than spinose. Tigers are, of course, crossbanded with dark pigment and pastels—well, that is pretty self-explanatory. Certainly, as linebreeding for specific colors is intensified, additional new patterns and colors will be forthcoming. I can only wonder how

Although a tail may help to secure a gecko on a perch, the lack of one does not prevent a crested gecko from climbing.

long it will be before an albino crested gecko is unexpectedly produced in someone's breeding program.

Color Changes

Since a certain degree of ontogenetic (age-related) color changes occur with this species, hatchlings or juveniles are invariably less colorful than the adults. Many months must pass before the lizards (or their keepers) realize their true color or pattern potential.

Crested Gecko Biology

Crested geckos derive both their common name and their scientific name of *ciliatus* from the crest of long, pointed scales (the supraciliaries) above each eye. Actually, long, pointed scales outline each side of the head. The crest scales (which become somewhat reduced in size on each shoulder) extend to a point on the sacrum (above the hind limbs).

The Tail

The crested gecko has a tail that is proportionately longer than that of many other species in the genus. It is 85 percent to 95 percent as long as the lizard's head and body. The tail is slender and cylindrical distally, and it becomes wider and flatter near the lizard's body. There are horizontal laminae containing setae beneath the broadened tail tip. The tail is moderately prehensile. Unfortunately, crested geckos lose (autotomize) their tail easily. If this happens when they are adult, the tail seldom regenerates. Juvenile examples are able to regenerate a broken tail reasonably well. When lost, the tail autotomizes at the base (just posterior to the hemipenial bulge).

Although the loss of a tail detracts considerably from the lizard's appearance in the eyes of many keepers, it does not seem to inhibit the gecko in any way.

Arboreal

The crested gecko is an arboreal species. Unlike the larger members of the genus that sit quietly on vertical tree trunks and on large horizontal limbs for hours on end, the crested gecko seems to prefer life among the smaller twigs. It is agile but not particularly speedy in its movements. When disturbed in the wild (or in walk-in cages when captive) the lizard usually simply moves upward to the next higher, secure perch.

Body Form

In keeping with the other species of the genus, crested geckos have broadly expanded toe tips beneath which are a series of undivided lamellae. Additionally, each of the four feet has extensive interdigital (between the toes) webbing. The webbing serves to make the feet look large and the toes seem short, but this is not actually the case.

Crested geckos and their relatives all have a stout body, and most of the species have a fold of skin from arms to groin low on each side. The lidless eye is covered with a transparent spectacle (the brille) and is cleaned frequently by the protrusible, slightly notched tongue. The pupils are narrowly elliptical by day or in bright light but are distended and almost round in darkness.

The raised superciliary scales of the crested gecko, *R. ciliatus*, are clearly visible.

Crested Gecko Relatives

Several different relatives of the crested gecko are available. The prices given are accurate as of this writing.

The Gargoyle Gecko

The gargoyle gecko, *Rhacodactylus auriculatus,* sells for between $40 and $150 each. Juveniles and those with the most bland or most common colors and patterns are less expensive than richly colored examples or adults. This species may be somewhat over 8.5 inches (22 cm) in total length when adult. Hatchlings are about 3 inches (7.5 cm) in length. It is a variably colored species. Some examples bear longitudinal stripes of dark brown (to almost black) against a ground color of gray. Others are prettily patterned in stripes or crossbars of rust red against a gray or a brown-and-gray background. Yet others may have a ground color of olive and a darker brown or olive-gray pattern of crossbars.

The Short-Snouted Giant Gecko

The short-snouted giant gecko, *Rhacodactylus chahoua,* is still uncommon in North American herpetoculture. When available, it sells for $350 to $800 each. This attractively colored and patterned gecko is often a moss green with mottling and blotches of lichen gray or vice versa. Other examples may have a lighter or darker ground color and a few may be almost orange or gray with orange highlights. It attains an adult length of about

R. auriculatus is popularly known as the gargoyle gecko.

R. chahoua, the short-snouted giant gecko, is now becoming popular with American hobbyists.

A portrait of the short-snouted giant gecko.

11 inches (28 cm). Hatchlings average about 4 inches (10 cm) in total length.

R. l. leachianus is the larger of the two subspecies, occasionally exceeding 12 inches (30 cm) in total length. Hatchlings are about 4.25 inches (10.8 cm) in total length. It is found on mainland New Caledonia and some nearby islets. It is usually a dark-colored gecko, being brown or gray with poorly defined and very irregular darker or moss green markings.

The smaller *R. l. henkeli* hails from Ile des Pins and is adult at about 10.5 inches (27 cm) in total length. Hatchlings are about the same size as those of the larger subspecies. This subspecies is lighter in color than the mainland form.

The New Caledonian Giant Gecko

The New Caledonian giant gecko, *Rhacodactylus leachianus,* occurs in two subspecies and many locality-specific insular forms. All have extraordinarily short tails. They sell for from $450 to $1,600 each.

This New Caledonian giant gecko has its original tail.

Many Sarasin's giant geckos are marked with a well-defined light bridle.

The Sarasin's Giant Gecko

Sarasin's giant gecko, *Rhacodactylus sarasinorum*, is adult at about 9.5 inches (24 cm) in total length. Hatchlings measure about 3.75 inches (9.5 cm) in total length. It currently sells for $250 to $500 each. The ground color varies from pale gray to chocolate-brown with an obscure to well-defined dorsal pattern. Darker markings may form vague crossbands, and a lighter vertebral stripe may be evident. The top of the head is often lighter than the body. A *V* of contrasting color (usually dark, occasionally light) runs from the eyes to where the lines converge on the shoulder.

The Rough-Snouted Giant Gecko

The rough-snouted giant gecko, *Rhacodactylus trachyrhynchus*, is another species to have two subspecies. *R. t. trachyrhynchus* is the highland form from mainland New Caledonia. It is adult at about 13 inches (33 cm) in length, of which almost half is tail length. Hatchlings are about 4.25 inches (10.8 cm) in total length. This species is a mossy green or brown with lighter lichenate markings. Although it is occasionally

bred in Europe, it is virtually unobtainable in the United States.

The other subspecies, *R. t. trachycephalus,* is found on Ile des Pins and is of a yellower ground coloration than the mainland form. Its greatest length seems to be about 11 inches (28 cm) and hatchlings are about 3.5 inches (9 cm) in length.

The rough-snouted giant gecko, *R. trachyrhynchus*, is the second largest of this New Caledonian genus.

Crested and Other Giant Geckos as Pets

The hobbyist must consider several factors before purchasing a gecko as a pet. How should a gecko be handled? How can one be obtained?

Choosing Your Giant Gecko

Although many reptiles and amphibians are chosen by hobbyists for the ease with which they can be handled or the fact that one species may be more easily fed or is more brightly colored than another, this is not the case at all with giant geckos. Since all of the species are relatively slow moving, any of them are relatively easy to handle. All require pretty much the same diet, so that is not a factor. Since none are clad in brilliant hues, color as a choice criterion cannot apply. Instead, with the giant geckos, choice of a species is based by many of us on cost, available space, and available species. Most casual hobbyists are unwilling to spend the several hundred dollars that a baby New Caledonian giant gecko would cost but feel that, at a cost of $50, a crested gecko or two is well worth the investment. Additionally, crested geckos are usually available while several other species may not be.

Terrarium cost (as well as the space needed for the terrarium) is much more modest for a 30-gallon (115-L) setup for one or two compatible crested geckos than for the 75-gallon (210-L) size that would eventually be needed for a New Caledonian giant gecko.

Terrarium Size

As you can see here, the greatest variables that you have to work with in selecting a species of giant gecko are your budget, the lizard's size, and the terrarium size. While you can certainly keep the small species in large cages, doing the opposite (keeping large species in small cages) is not an option. Also, if you decide to keep several giant geckos rather than just one, the terrarium required will necessarily be larger. Choose wisely.

Terrarium Orientation

Keep in mind that giant geckos are arboreal lizards, and their needs will be best served if they are housed in vertically oriented terraria. Thus, when considering the space in which to place your terrarium, you will not have to allocate the full 48 × 18 inches (120 × 45 cm) usually needed for a conventionally oriented 75-gallon (210-L) tank. Rather, by placing the tank vertically, you will need only the horizontal space for a small end. Remember also that whether horizontal or vertical, the terrarium must be tightly covered.

Handling Your Crested and Giant Geckos

Although giant geckos are alert, none among their ranks are particularly fast. Be that as it may, to a giant gecko, whether newly imported or a long-term captive, an approaching hand usually equates to grave danger. Few geckos will simply sit quietly and allow themselves to be lifted and handled. I feel strongly that geckos—all geckos, not just the giants—are not pets in the traditional handleable manner. They are lizards for you to observe, appreciate, and learn from, not lizards that are to be handled at whim. In fact, if I were asked for a single phrase that best fitted geckos as pets it would be "just look, don't touch."

How to Handle
When it does become necessary to handle your giant geckos, do so firmly but gently. Allowing them to squirm in your grasp will only accentuate the possibility of injuring their skin or breaking their tail. If

Two handfuls of New Caledonian giant geckos.

their skin is torn, most tears will heal over quickly. Even quite considerable scars will heal almost imperceptibly after a lizard sheds its skin several times.

Biting Hazard
Giant geckos of all kinds can and may bite. Although a bite by a crested gecko or one of its smaller relatives would be little more than a pinch, a bite from the largest species, *R. leachianus*, can be a painful and not soon forgotten experience. A giant gecko's defensive tactics usually begin with the lizard tensing. If the disturbance persists, this is followed by a hoarse bark, a lunge, and a bite—a hard bite.

Moving Geckos
If you choose not to grasp your giant geckos, they may be moved in other ways. If you are moving them from a smaller to a larger cage, you can simply place the former into the latter and remove the top from or open the door of the smaller one. Then secure the larger one, and let the geckos move out at their own speed. A second

A large, tailless male crested gecko. The tail will not regenerate.

This pretty crested gecko is preparing to leap to another leaf.

way is to place a large cup or small plastic pail over them. You can then slide a piece of rigid plastic or cardboard over the top of the pail and move each lizard without ever actually touching it.

Observing Your Geckos

When they feel secure, giant geckos are not at all secretive. Depending on the species, some will sit preferentially in a head-down position on a vertical log, on the terrarium glass, or on a stalk of bamboo. Others situate themselves horizontally on elevated limbs. Some species may perch amid the thinner limbs of a woody potted plant. By the prudent positioning of each gecko's favorite perch, you should be able to keep your giant geckos visible at all times.

Of course, when first placed into a terrarium, it is not unusual for a giant gecko to seclude itself immediately and to remain hidden for hours or days until it feels secure in its new surroundings. Once it feels at home, the lizard will begin emerging from its temporary sanctuary, sometimes slowly, sometimes quickly, and it will soon choose a basking perch to which it will return time and again. Initially, even though the gecko is used to its quarters, it still may rotate out of sight as you approach but will eventually become fully used to its surroundings and to your motions outside of the cage.

Obtaining Your Crested or Giant Gecko

Since the habitats and populations of many species of geckos are diminishing and since all giant geckos are considered vulnerable, few of these lizards are collected from the wild. If you are given the choice between a wild-collected or a captive-bred and hatched specimen, choose the latter. Not only are they apt to be better adjusted at the time of purchase, your purchase of captive-bred specimens is a positive statement for herpetoculture and a positive step for conservation.

Characteristics to Consider

You should consider certain things when deciding whether to purchase a crested or giant gecko. The gecko you select should be stocky, alert, active, have all of its fingers and toes, not have open wounds, and not have sunken eyes. The sacrum should not appear bony and protruding. Whether you select one with a broken or regenerated tail will be largely up to you. Neither of the latter is particularly serious, but keep in mind that giant geckos are not as apt to regenerate their tails as are geckos from some other genera. Do not select an obviously undernourished

When hanging from a perch, crested geckos help support themselves with their prehensile tail.

This young crested gecko is redder than most.

gecko or one with loose stools or with feces smeared at the anal opening. If the gecko you select has been collected from the wild, you may wish to have fecal smears done by a veterinarian to determine gut parasite type and load. Do not choose a gecko that seems thin but has stocky hind limbs (an early indicator of MBD, see pages 35–36).

Most of the crested and giant geckos in the pet trade are now captive bred. This preponderance of captive-bred specimens speaks well for not only the hardiness and adaptability of the giant geckos but for the ever-increasing knowledge and diligence of hobbyists and commercial reptile breeders.

Where to Find Geckos

World Wide Web: Crested geckos and other species of giant geckos are often advertised on the World Wide Web, which has within the last few years become an important source of information. By instructing your search engine to seek *giant geckos* or a specific kind of giant gecko (such as crested geckos or gargoyle geckos) you should be referred to the web sites of many breeders and dealers. Many have excellent photos (often of the example being offered) on their web sites. Reptile-oriented classified ads in hobbyist magazines are also excellent sources.

Local pet stores and local breeders are excellent sources of crested geckos and occasionally of related species as well. There you can see the animals, discuss them freely with personnel, personally assess each lizard's health, and watch them feed and interact.

There may be some questions that your local pet shop is unable to answer. Among these will be the origin of a given wild-collected specimen or the history and genetics of a specific giant gecko. In most cases, the history of a gecko becomes irretrievably lost once the animal enters the commercial pet trade. The single exception to this will be the records available from breeders, should you decide to buy direct.

Herp expos: In many areas of the world, herp expos are now held on a regular basis. In the United States, they are held in many of our larger cities. Some occur annually, some quarterly, and some monthly. The expos are usually well advertised in the various reptile magazines and on a number of web sites.

An expo is merely a gathering of dealers and breeders, all under one roof. Expos vary in size from the 650+ tables of Wayne Hill's National Reptile Breeders' Expo, which is held in Florida every August, to some that, although much smaller, are quite comprehensive. Not only are the more common species of giant geckos well represented at most of these shows,

A pretty crested gecko rests on an inclined limb.

This is a heavy-bodied female crested gecko.

but occasionally true rarities may be found. Support equipment—terraria, cage furniture, and the like—is often also available. Breeders usually offer parasite-free, well-acclimated specimens and accurate information. Most keep records of genetics, lineage, fecundity, health, or quirks of the species with which they work and especially of the specimens in their breeding programs.

Reptile dealers have existed at least since the 1940s. Besides often breeding fair numbers of the reptiles they offer, specialty dealers deal directly with other breeders (across the world) and may even be direct importers of wild-collected species not yet being captive bred. Many such dealers both buy and sell reptiles and amphibians at herp expos.

Herpetological clubs also exist in many cities. You can learn about them by asking at pet stores, museums, college biology departments, or some high schools. At these meetings, if queried, fellow enthusiasts may be able to offer comments about some reptile dealers.

Mail-Order Purchase and Shipping

Even today, with herp expos and expanded neighborhood pet stores now the norm, the species of giant gecko in which you are interested may not be locally available. If this is the case, mail order may be the answer.

First you must find the gecko, then you must contact the advertiser. From the advertiser you should learn about the gecko's feeding habits, age, and other pertinent information.

Shipping decisions: The shipping of reptiles is not at all the insurmountable barrier that many hobbyists initially think it to be. However, it can be expensive. The chances are excellent that the supplier that you have chosen to use is quite familiar with shipping and will be delighted to assist you in any way possible.

Among the things about which you and your shipper will have to agree is the method of payment and the method and date of shipping. The shipping is most safely accomplished when outdoor temperatures are moderate.

The dual crests of the crested gecko extend from above the eye to the sacral area.

Lizards may be shipped in a number of ways. Discuss the pros and cons of each with your shipper. Today there is a growing tendency to use the door-to-door services of carriers such as USPS, UPS, and FedEx. These are less expensive and often faster than traditional airport-to-airport airline service.

Methods of shipping: Options are available for shipping lizards that are not available for shipping snakes or turtles. Some include the following.

- **Express Mail (USPS):** This is usually a door-to-door prepaid service for which your shipper will require payment in advance. The cost is $15 to $25.
- **Air Freight** is an airport-to-airport service. Depending on the airline used, either two or three levels of service are available. Regular, space-available freight with charges collect costs about $35. Air express, guaranteed flights, with charges collect costs about $70. Special handling, guaranteed flights, with charges prepaid costs about $70.
- **Other Options:** Occasionally, shipping companies such as Airborne or FedEx will accept lizards (this is the

local manager's prerogative). Charges may usually be either prepaid or collect and cost between $25 and $50 for this door-to-door service.

Someone must usually be at home to sign for the package on any of the door-to-door services.

Payment: Increasingly, payment requested by shippers is for both the animal(s) and their shipping. Unless the shipper knows you well, you will have to pay in advance (including boxing charges if any) before the animal(s) will be shipped to you. This usually means a money order, cashier's check, credit card, or wire transfer of funds. Many shippers will accept personal checks but will not ship until the check has cleared their bank (usually a week or so after deposit).

An alternate method of payment is COD (collect on delivery). However, because of a hefty COD surcharge, this can be expensive and is often inconvenient.

Details: To ship, your supplier will need your full name, address and current day and night telephone numbers. Agree on a shipping date. If you elect to use airport-to-airport

A female crested gecko poses on a lichen-clad branch.

service, specify which airport you wish to use.

Shipping by any service on weekends, holidays, or during very hot or very cold weather may be difficult and should be discouraged. If applicable, pick up your shipment as quickly after its arrival as possible. This is especially important in bad weather. Learn the hours of your cargo office and whether the shipment can be picked up at the ticket counter if it arrives after the cargo office has closed.

You will have to pay for your shipment (including all COD charges and fees) before you can inspect it. Once you are given your shipment, open and inspect it before leaving the cargo facility.

Unless otherwise specified, reliable shippers guarantee live delivery. However, to substantiate the existence of a problem, both shippers and airlines will require a discrepancy or damage report be made out, signed, and dated by airline personnel. In the very rare case when a problem has occurred, insist on the filling out and filing of a claim form and contact your shipper immediately for instructions.

Hopefully, after the first time, you will no longer find the shipping of specimens intimidating. Understanding the system will open wide new doors of acquisition.

Robust and healthy, this male crested gecko lacks both tail and bright colors.

Caging

Crested geckos and their relatives are hardy and easily kept. They are nocturnal lizards that should be provided with some manner of darkened, elevated shelter in which they may escape the glare of electric lights or sunlight. The size of the cage and the furniture it contains will necessarily vary by the size, the number, and the habits of the geckos you intend to house. As long as basics are met, giant geckos may be kept in intricate terraria, simple terraria, large wood and wire cages, or even suitably appointed, escape-proof greenhouses.

Cage Basics

None of the giant geckos tolerate crowding well. Since several of the species have been known to interbreed, it is best to keep each species separated from others. Males of all species of giant geckos fight persistently and savagely with other males. It is usually not possible to keep more than one male in an enclosure, even if many visual barriers are incorporated and the cage is large. Females are less combative, and from one to several can usually be kept with a single male.

This simple crested gecko cage contains egg crate hiding areas, an egg-deposition box, a water dish, and some food.

Females may spar a little and establish a hierarchy but are usually compatible. Newly introduced adult males and females may occasionally fight and require monitoring for their first few nights together.

Hatchlings and juveniles may usually be maintained together but must be watched for squabbling. This monitoring becomes more important as they near sexual maturity. After then, baby males in a group setting will become adversarial.

Terrarium Size

For a pair or trio of small to medium-sized giant geckos (including crested geckos), a 40-gallon (150-L) terrarium (16 × 16 × 36 inches [40 × 40 × 90 cm]) or cage of equal dimensions will pro-

Sarasin's giant gecko is a small member of the genus.

Even though horizontally oriented, this is a simple but effective crested gecko terrarium.

terrarium is oriented in a standard manner and is of a standard shape, covering it is a simple matter. Clip-on screen or wire mesh tops with either molded plastic or galvanized frames are readily available at many pet stores. Tightly covering your terrarium if you have oriented it vertically (as suggested) or if it is an odd shape can be more problematic.

A metal-framed wire top can be used for a vertically oriented terrarium, provided the end on which the tank rests is lifted at least 0.5 inches (1 cm) above the stand on which it sits. This can be accomplished by placing the tank atop strategically placed 1 × 2 inch (2.5 × 5 cm) boards. A standard top can then be clipped in place using standard top clips.

Reptile tanks with built-in sliding screen tops are now rather readily available in many pet stores. These screen tops slide open and closed on molded plastic frames that are permanently affixed to the terrarium. They work well no matter the orientation of the terrarium. The tops close tightly and are lockable. We consider

vide sufficient space. Stand the tank on end to provide adequate height for these arboreal lizards. For a pair or trio of the large species, we suggest nothing of less size than a 75-gallon (285-L) terrarium, again standing on end. A tank of this size measures approximately 18 × 18 × 48 inches (45 × 45 × 180 cm). If constrained too tightly, giant geckos may survive but will not thrive. There will also be an unnatural amount of squabbling in a group. Because giant geckos are persistently arboreal, I suggest using a vertically oriented terrarium.

Safety and Security Issues

Giant geckos will escape if able but are not as accomplished escape artists as some other gecko species. Their terrarium, no matter its shape, must be tightly and totally covered. If your

The transverse lamellae on the forefoot of this New Caledonian giant gecko, *R. leachianus*, are clearly visible.

these terraria an excellent choice for housing giant geckos. Other tanks are available with screen-covered ventilation holes about 2 inches (5 cm) in diameter that are drilled through the glass tank ends. Adequate ventilation is very important to all reptiles, especially in areas where the weather is perpetually hot and humid.

Other Terrarium Considerations

A very workable terrarium that has been designed primarily for chameleons is now being commercially produced and is available at many pet stores. This unit has a glass front and bottom and has screen ends, back, and top. The frame is lightweight plastic, and the top easily slides open and is lockable when closed. The screen provides excellent air circulation, and may in fact allow the tank to get too dry in areas where humidity is naturally low.

When a tank is vertically oriented, one of the small glass ends becomes

the top. If you use a heat lamp, do not put the bulb against the glass of the tank or the glass will break. We put the bulbs into a metal, round reflector and hold the unit about an inch (2.5 cm) above the glass by affixing alligator paper clips around the edge of the reflector. Remember also that the glass will filter out the UV rays that you are striving to provide for the geckos.

Some Caging Basics

Giant geckos are persistently arboreal. Although they are perfectly capable of clinging to vertical trunks and limbs, and will often position themselves head downward on these, we suggest that the perches in terraria and cages be more diagonally or horizontally oriented. Illuminate and warm at least one of the horizontal perches (preferably two) from above to provide a suitable area for thermoregulation. Sections of giant bamboo or cork tubing are ideal perch material. In a glass terrarium, tank length sections can be held in place by a dollop of latex aquarium sealant on each end. If you are keeping more than a single giant gecko per terrarium, provide visual barriers. Since the dominant gecko in any group will claim the most prominent and satisfactory basking spot, it is important to provide two or more areas conducive to each gecko's thermoregulation.

Giant geckos prefer to drink by lapping pendulous droplets of water from freshly misted plant leaves or bamboo sections. Unless the water surface is roiled with the bubbles from an aquarium air stone (driven by a small vibrator pump), many giant

This is a small planted terrarium.

If the terrarium is in a particularly warm area, you might consider placing a small fan just above the tank with its airflow directed just over the top of terrarium, not into the setup. This will provide a gentle but perpetual air movement that will help control humidity and stagnation.

Adjusting Cage Humidity

Crested and other giant geckos dwell in humid forest habitats. Captives are quite tolerant of most caging situations but it is best to meet or exceed certain minimum criteria. Among other factors such as temperature, the issue of humidity should also be addressed.

Increasing Humidity

A cage can be made more humid by restricting airflow in some manner. In a normal glass-sided terrarium, restricting airflow may be accomplished by removing a terrarium-top fan if one is in place or by covering a portion of a screen or wire top with

geckos will steadfastly refuse to drink from a water dish. Mist the leaves of your plants with tepid water daily. Be certain that your terrarium plants have not been freshly sprayed with insecticides or liquid fertilizers. Grow commercially procured plants for a couple of weeks outside of the terrarium to allow systemic additives a chance to dissipate. To grow in a terrarium, most plants (even forest plants) will need strong lighting. Suitable lighting can be provided by using an incandescent plant grow or a UV heat bulb. Although it is uncertain whether full-spectrum lighting actually benefits these nocturnal geckos in any way, neither will it hurt them. I suggest that one be provided, if only for a few hours a day.

A portrait of a New Caledonian giant gecko.

A Terrarium Suggestion for Crested Geckos

Beautiful terraria may be made for giant geckos by converting hexagonal aquariums to terraria. The two sizes that I have used most successfully are of 40-gallon (150-L) and of 65-gallon (250-L) capacity. Although molded plastic tops are available specifically for these tanks, we prefer to use custom-made wire tops that will allow a suitable air exchange.

A trio of small to medium-sized giant geckos can be maintained successfully in the 40-gallon (150-L) arrangement and a pair of the true giants in the larger 65-gallon (250-L) setup. Illumination may be provided by a fluorescent fixture fitted with a full-spectrum bulb, by an incandescent UV-A and heat flood light, or by both. The UV-A plus heat flood light combination provides warmth as well as UV and normal light. Cage furniture will necessarily vary according to the kind of geckos kept within. A place of security created by one or two large-diameter, vertically oriented hollow logs or cork bark tubes will be utilized.

Plant suggestions: Additional visual barriers created from crisscrossed bamboo stems or growing plants will add to the lizard's feeling of security and the beauty of the terrarium. Suggested plants are *Epipremnum aureum* (pothos or variegated philodendron), sansevierias of various forms, and nonspinose bromeliads for larger gecko species. To these you may add a robust potted *Ficus benjamina* (Benjamin's fig) for crested geckos to climb on. You can shop for terrarium plants on the Web.

Feeding issues: An elevated feeding platform should be provided. On this the gecko's daily dishful of vitamin-enhanced fruit-honey mixture may be placed. Since large geckos can be rather clumsy when eating, an edging around the feeding shelf that will prevent the dish from being knocked off will eliminate much mess. The plants can be misted daily to provide moisture for the geckos, but truthfully, the lizards derive much of their water requirements from the liquefied honey-fruit mixture.

Other considerations: A substrate of several inches of potting soil (plain, not the kind with Styrofoam beads or time-release fertilizer!) will provide rooting material for potted plants. Bromeliads may be carefully wired to the upright cork or limb well above the soil.

Adult female giant geckos will usually descend to the soil to lay their periodic clutches of two eggs. They may use any area of the substrate having suitable temperature and moisture content (including inside their log or cork tube if an open end rests on the soil) for the deposition site. Small cage bird nesting boxes containing about 2 inches (5 cm) of potting soil will also be used by these lizards. Depending on the species and the health of your females, from five to nine clutches will be laid annually at roughly 30-day intervals. I suggest that the eggs be moved to an incubator as soon after laying as possible. This will eliminate the possibility of accidental damage from the adult geckos during the 60- to 75-day (occasionally longer) incubation time.

plastic film or glass. This, of course, also retains more heat if a heater is in use. If you have a screen-sided terrarium, it may be necessary to tape plastic film over one or more of the sides before humidity will begin to rise. Humidity may also be raised by replacing a small water bowl with one that has a large surface area or by placing the existing water bowl over a heat tape. Keep in mind that heated water evaporates more quickly than cool water and you will have to check the water level in the bowl frequently. Live plants, especially live tropical plants such as bromeliads, that hold water in a central cup will also elevate cage humidity. Misting the plants frequently will help even more. If you dwell in a desert or other arid region, you may have to combine several of the above techniques to create and retain a satisfactorily high humidity in your gecko's cage.

Decreasing Humidity

Conversely, if you live in a fog belt or in the perpetually humid southeastern United States, you may desire to reduce cage humidity. Reverse the above procedures to accomplish this. By providing greater airflow and reducing the size of any water-holding receptacle kept in the terrarium, humidity will be reduced somewhat. Keeping the terrarium in an air-conditioned room will reduce humidity dramatically, so much in fact that you may need to institute one or more

of the humidity-elevating techniques previously discussed.

Greenhouses

Greenhouses of many styles, constructed from several types of materials, are readily available today. These vary from simple, self-standing, fully constructed types available from dealers of storage sheds through myriad do-it-yourself kits to elaborate and decorative commercial kinds that, unless you are very handy, are best left to contractor setup. Greenhouses are becoming ever more popular and can be ideal homes for giant geckos, at least during the summer months. Some thought must be given to keeping these lizards in greenhouses in cold climates because they often cling to the glass. The frosty glass panes of winter can cause the loss of toes or feet or even the death of the giant gecko. Cage the geckos to keep them off of the glass during winter.

Some gargoyle geckos are blotched with orange.

Greenhouses with double glazing are better, safer, and far more economical (after the initial purchase price) than single-glazed structures. Greenhouses are usually considered permanent structures, and a building permit is required to install one legally.

Safety Issues

Heating and cooling units and windows must be entirely screened from the inside to prevent injury to, or escape of, the gecko inhabitants. It is important to secure even those fixtures well above ground level. The base of a greenhouse must be flush against a concrete slab, affixed to a concrete or brick (stem) wall, or be sunk a foot (30 cm) or more below the surface of the ground. This will preclude easy access by outside predators and escape by the creatures with which you are working.

Greenhouse Additions

Heated greenhouses typically exemplify the adage that the grass is always greener elsewhere and can bring a few square feet of the tropics to the snowbelt or the desert. If you are a purist, a greenhouse would allow you to grow some of the New Caledonian plants among which giant geckos are found in the wild (New Caledonian plant species can be researched on the Web). Again, before making your purchase, research all aspects of the greenhouse itself as well as the appropriate heating, cooling, misting, and ventilation systems. One kind may suit your needs far better than another. When providing furniture, affix rocks or tree trunks solidly to prevent one from moving and injuring the geckos or actually damaging the greenhouse. The possibility, and feasibility, of providing a small pond and waterfall, often much-wanted accoutrements, should be well thought out at the outset. Ponds and waterfalls can be wonderful and feasible additions to a rain forest theme that would be impossible to construct in any other setting.

When approached with imagination and forethought, the interior of even a small greenhouse, whether of a lean-to or a free-standing style, can become the focal point of your home and a wonderful home for your geckos.

This half-grown New Caledonian giant gecko has a regenerated tail.

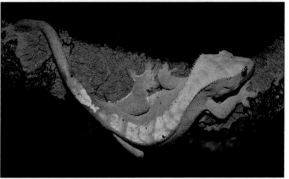

This crested gecko is well anchored with tail and feet on the side of a limb.

The Role of UV Lighting

We now understand the role that UV-A and UV-B waves play with diurnal reptiles rather well. However, we are still speculating on their role with nocturnal species. UV waves are an actual necessity when you are raising numbers of day geckos. Do they really help in the day-to-day care of night-active giant geckos? We just do not know. However, we hypothesize that UV will not hurt the lizards and so suggest their use.

In the wild, the synthesizing of vitamin D_3, which assists in the metabolizing of calcium, is aided when a lizard basks in unfiltered sunlight and avails itself of the ultraviolet wave UV-B. Additionally, the wavelength UV-A promotes natural behavior by herps. However, do nocturnal geckos normally bask enough to benefit from unfiltered sunlight? We simply do not know.

Besides natural sunlight and full-spectrum cage lighting, calcium can be provided in dietary form. Food insects can be sprinkled with a powdered calcium-D_3 supplement and liquid calcium-D_3 can be given to the omnivorous giant geckos in the babyfood-honey mixture that should be an integral part of their diet (see page 31). There are some indications that not all reptiles utilize it well when it is given in this way, but in most cases it seems to work ideally.

However, it must be mentioned that there *can* be too much of a good thing. Since UV-B actually stimulates the synthesizing of D_3, when a high-quality UV-B-emitting bulb or natural sunlight is provided, the D_3-calcium supplements should be correspondingly reduced. Sadly, there is no formula for determining the amount or frequency with which supplements should be provided. Use care, and observe your pet frequently.

Suggestions for a Movable, Outdoor Crested and Giant Gecko Cage

Although giant geckos are nocturnal, they thrive in outside cages (constructed of 1/8-inch [3-mm] hardware cloth) in warm climates. Access to unfiltered sunshine, rainfall, and an entirely natural photoperiod can be nothing but beneficial.

Because my breeding facility was located in sunny and almost perpetually hot southwest Florida, I was able to keep most geckos outside for more than 10 months of each year. Large casters were attached to the bottom to facilitate ease of cage movement. This allowed us to move the cages with the seasons, spreading them out beneath the shade trees for the spring, summer, and autumn and bringing them closely together in sunny areas during the winter. The cages had a bottom and top of 3/4-inch (2 cm) exterior plywood and were framed with pressure-treated 2 × 2s (5 × 5 cm wood). The 1/8-inch (3 mm) mesh hardware cloth was chosen because it prevents the escape of all but the smallest-size crickets.

Dimensions: The outside dimensions of the cage (including the casters) were 72 inches (183 cm) high by 48 inches (122 cm) long by 32 inches (81 cm) wide. This allowed the cages to be rolled inside through sliding patio doors if the weather became really cold for an extended period. The dimensions of the hinged, front-opening, door were 24 inches (61 cm) wide by 48 inches (122 cm) high. The wire is stapled to the frame using stainless 3/8-inch-long (1-cm) staples from a standard, hand-powered staple gun. Those staples that do not seat tightly are tapped in with a hammer.

Inside the enclosure: Cage furniture includes a potted ficus tree, a number of diagonal and horizontal branches, tubes of cork bark, and hanging pots of vining philodendrons. Fifty pounds (22 kg) of potting soil–play sand mixture was spread around the bottom of the cage. Although some washes through the wire with each rainstorm or cage cleaning, the sand lasts for several weeks before needing replacing.

Cleaning the cage: On the rare occasions when the cages needed a thorough cleaning, the lizards are removed; the uprights, top, and bottom are scrubbed with a dilute bleach solution; then the whole cage is hosed thoroughly with a garden hose. New substrate is then provided. Between the thorough cleanings, the cages are misted for about a half an hour daily. During the winter months the cages are covered with 4-mil plastic sheeting. This is stapled firmly in place over three sides and the top. The top sheet of plastic is fitted around and above the cage's heat lamp. The front of the cage is covered with a separate sheet of plastic that is stapled only at the top to allow it to be rolled up when the weather is sufficiently warm.

This arrangement works well until the outside temperature drops to very low 40°F (5–8°C). If it is colder than that, the cages must be rolled indoors.

Feeding

As mentioned earlier, giant geckos have complex (but, fortunately, rather easily duplicated) diets. They not only consume insects but also seek out nectars, pollens, exudates from over-ripe fruits, and the fruits themselves. Items such as mashed banana, mashed kiwi fruit, and bottled fruit nectar may be offered.

Supplements

The fondness of giant geckos for sweet fruit products offers you a simple way of administering the necessary vitamin and mineral supplements as well. Without the latter, especially vitamin D_3 and calcium, giant geckos are quite apt to develop a metabolic bone disorder (once simply called decalcification or rubber bone disease). Female geckos that are utilizing calcium to form shells for their developing eggs and rapidly growing young will be affected more quickly (and will therefore require more calcium) than adult males or nonovulating females.

Ideally, the ratio of calcium to phosphorus should be 2 to 1, and the ratio of vit-amin D_3 to vitamin A should be 1 to 1. A lack of D_3 (D_3 enhances calcium metabolism) or an excess of vitamin A can cause skeletal demineralization and deformities. Conversely, an excess of vitamin D_3 can allow over-metabolizing of calcium and the resulting visceral gout. In captivity, the prudent use of vitamin/mineral supplements is necessary even with full-spectrum lighting. However, the lizards' D_3 intake can be greatly reduced if the geckos are kept outside and allowed access to natural, unfiltered sunlight.

How Much and How Often

Our feeding regimen provides fruit-honey mixture at all times and

A portrait of a crested gecko.

How to Make Fruit-Honey Mixture for Your Giant Geckos

Mix

1/3 of a small jar of pureed papaya, apricot, peach, or mixed fruit baby food (to this some hobbyists add a bit of pureed turkey)
1 tablespoon of honey
1/3 eyedropper of Avitron liquid bird vitamins
1/2 teaspoon of Osteoform or Reptivite powdered vitamins
Add enough water to make this mixture a soupy consistency
1/2 tablespoon of bee pollen can be added if available

Feed this mixture as needed in elevated dishes. Do not smear it onto the terrarium glass for there it will solidify into an almost impossible-to-remove sheet. Refrigerate the food not used, but discard and remake it after one week. Replace the mixture in the cage daily. Many breeders feed this mixture to their baby crested (and other giant) geckos daily but provide it to half-grown and adult geckos only twice or thrice weekly.

gut-loaded insects every second day. The insects are simply dropped into the geckos' terrarium. The size of the insects necessarily varies with the size of the geckos being fed. Three-inch-long (7.5 cm) juvenile giant geckos require fly-sized (or smaller) crickets, while the 9-inch (23 cm) to 14-inch-long (36 cm) adults relish larger insects.

High-Quality Foods

You can control the quality of the food insects you offer your giant geckos. A poorly fed insect offers little but bulk as a food item. In contrast, a food insect that has been fed a variety of nutritious foods, particularly just before being offered as food to your

This crested gecko is cleaning its brille (spectacle).

This crested gecko has the crests highlighted in off-white.

insectivorous lizards, is a nutritional bonus package.

Foods to offer your feed insects include calcium, vitamin D_3, fresh fruit, grated carrots, squash, broccoli, fresh alfalfa and/or bean sprouts, honey, vitamin/mineral-enhanced (chick) laying mash, and high-quality tropical fish foods. A commercially prepared cricket gut-loading diet is now commercially available. This can also be used for mealworms and king mealworms.

This is a blotched example of the gargoyle gecko.

Food insects that are commercially available include crickets, mealworms, giant mealworms, wax worms, fruit flies, houseflies, silkworms, and trevoworms (butter worms). Variety is good for your lizards. Also consider offering to giant geckos nonnoxious field plankton, insects that you gather from the wild with a sweep net (discard spiders, bees, hornets (and other stinging insects), and hairy caterpillars). Choose an area free from insecticide and fertilizers when gathering field plankton. If you need large numbers of commercially bred insects, get dealers' names and phone numbers from the classified ads in reptile magazines or check the Web. The latter often provides instant online ordering opportunities as well. If you need only small numbers of feed insects, your local pet or feed store may be your most economical source.

A very occasional pinkie (newborn or slightly larger) mouse is often relished by larger giant geckos.

Health

If they are fed and housed properly, giant geckos of all species are very trouble-free, long-lived lizards. However, medical problems requiring the assessment and intervention of a veterinarian may arise occasionally. Not all veterinarians are comfortable treating reptiles, nor are all qualified to do so. You should locate a suitable veterinarian and discuss your lizards with him/her before veterinary services are actually needed. Reptile-qualified veterinarians now often advertise their expertise in the yellow pages of your local phone book and in trade magazines. Veterinarian referral services are also available. Members of your local herpetological society may also be able to suggest a qualified veterinarian.

Quarantine: To prevent the possible spread of diseases and parasites between giant geckos, you must quarantine newly acquired specimens (one to a tank) for a given period of time. A week would be the minimum time, a month would be much better. During this time, each quarantined gecko should be in a cage by itself, and you should be carefully sterilizing your hands and any equipment you may use between cages. The quarantine area should be completely removed from the area in which other reptiles are kept, preferably in another room.

Each quarantine tank should be thoroughly cleaned and sterilized prior to the introduction of the new lizard, and it should be regularly cleaned throughout the quarantine period. As with any other terrarium, the quarantine tank should be geared to the needs of the specimen that it is to house. Temperature, humidity, size, lighting, and all other factors must be considered.

During quarantine, take the time just to watch your lizard for any abnormal behavior. Fecal exams should be carried out to determine whether or not endoparasites are present. For this, you simply take a fresh stool sample to your reptile veterinarian. Only after you are completely satisfied that your new specimen is healthy and habituated should it be brought near other specimens.

Respiratory ailments: Giant geckos are not particularly prone to respiratory ailments of any kind. Should one occur, though, it can quickly debilitate a choice specimen. Respiratory ailments can be caused by overly damp and cold shipping or caging conditions or by other kinds of improper husbandry. Respiratory ailments can be of viral or bacterial origin and will require nasal or mucal swabs to determine the sensitivity of the causative agents to a particular

The undersurface of the hind foot of a crested gecko.

medication. A giant gecko suffering from a respiratory problem may display labored breathing through a partially opened mouth. Consult a veterinarian. While awaiting a medical opinion, provide your gecko with a thermal gradient, elevating and maintaining the cage temperature at one end of the terrarium to 90–95°F (32–35°C) around the clock (unless your veterinarian directs otherwise).

Torn skin: In comparison with the integument of some other geckos, the skin of a giant gecko is quite tough. However, abrasions, tears, and cuts can still occur. Most of these are husbandry related—two males being kept together, sharp edges on cage furniture, or very rough handling. Two male giant geckos should never be housed together. Bruises and small tears will heal and may become almost invisible after a few sheds. Large tears may require veterinary assessment and intervention. Tears, cuts, and abrasions should be carefully watched for infection and an antibiotic cream be applied if necessary.

Mouth rot: Infectious stomatitis is another malady that is rarely seen in giant geckos. It is caused by bruising of the snout and mouth. If present, the soft tissue will be puffy, soft, and discolored, and a cheesy exudate may be present between the teeth. If left untreated, this can cause jawbone deterioration, tooth loss, and eventual death. Neosporin and/or sulfa drugs are the medications of choice. However, if a positive response is not quickly seen, consult your veterinarian.

Broken tail: Giant geckos autotomize their tail with remarkable ease. Although in some cases the tail may regenerate, it often does not. Tail loss may be disconcerting to the keeper and disfiguring to the gecko, but it is not health threatening. Never grasp your gecko by its tail.

Floppy-tail syndrome: This unsightly problem occurs occasionally in many gecko species. Although the tail looks normal when the gecko is ascending or level atop a limb, it bends abruptly upward at the base when the lizard is inverted or descending a vertical surface. The cause of this is unknown. However, it may pertain to improper calcium utilization or a weak joint structure. The syndrome is uncorrectable.

Metabolic bone disease (MBD): This is a symptom rather than a disease. The actual disease is more correctly known as hypoparathyroidism. Giant geckos are especially prone to MBD. This is an insidious disease that is caused by improper nutrition, specifically by too little dietary calcium or, if calcium is present in suitable amounts, by the inability of the lizard to metabolize it properly. The role of ultraviolet light, vitamin D_3, and calcium is discussed in detail in the caging section on page 29. MBD is characterized by pliable bones, swollen legs, and a foreshortened or puffy look to the face. In its early stages, the progression can be halted but not reversed. Generally, any physical disfigurements attributable to MBD are there to stay. By providing the needed calcium in the lizard's diet, the onset of MBD can be negated entirely.

Stress: If giant geckos are overcrowded, kept too cool, kept too hot, or subjected to aggression by dominant terrarium mates, they will display certain signs of stress. Among these are a tendency for the subordinate specimen(s) to hide continually, to feed poorly or not at all, to be continually fearful and nervous, and to display an abnormal coloration (usually dark) persistently. Stress can prove fatal to an otherwise healthy gecko. Observe your geckos frequently, and learn their normal colors and reactions. Stress may be reduced by adding visual barriers, by placing your animals into a larger cage, by adjusting cage temperature, or by adding additional females. If after all of these corrective measures stress continues, you will have no choice but to separate your specimens into individual terraria. If this becomes necessary, it is

usually possible to move the male to the female's container periodically (and temporarily) for the purpose of breeding. Watch carefully for signs of overt aggressiveness by and toward any geckos kept in a communal setup. Be prepared to take whatever corrective actions that may be necessary.

Skin shedding: All lizards shed their skin. The process is termed *ecdysis*. Shedding occurs with more frequency during periods of fast growth or to repair skin damage. Shedding results from thyroid activity. As the old keratinous layer loosens from the new one forming beneath it, your giant gecko may dull in color. The shedding gecko usually eats its discarded skin. When shedding has been completed, your specimen will again be as (or more) brightly colored and patterned as it was before the process began.

If your giant gecko experiences problems shedding, the cause is usually because the lizard is dehydrated or in otherwise suboptimal condition or because the humidity in the terrarium/cage is too low. When shedding problems occur, they are most often associated with toes and tail tips. Although giant geckos are adept at removing these problematic pieces themselves, if they do not succeed, then their keeper

must intervene very carefully. Leaving dried skin in place can result in toe or tail tip loss. If patches of skin adhere, a gentle misting with tepid water or a daub of mineral oil from a Q-tip may help make removal easier.

When shedding, crested geckos look rather tattered.

The tongue may be used to help dislodge the remaining facial skin.

Skin infections: These are not common but may occur if a giant gecko's terrarium is too humid. Infections may also occur at an injury site. Altering terrarium/cage humidity is a simple process, but veterinary assistance may be required to cure the infection.

Broken limbs and other physical injuries: Injuries such as these may occur if your giant gecko is dropped, if it falls, if it jumps from a moderate height, or if it is involved in a fight. These injuries can also happen if the gecko is trapped beneath or in back of a shifting piece of heavy cage furniture. If severe enough to be at all debilitating, veterinary assessment should be sought immediately.

Internal parasites (endoparasites): Although giant geckos do not seem plagued by endoparasites, some may harbor these pests. Endoparasites may not always require treatment. However, if they cause bloody stools or other intestinal discomfort, they will need to be addressed. Because of the complexities of identifying endoparasites and the necessity to weigh specimens accurately to treat them and to measure purge dosages, the eradication of internal parasites is best left to a qualified reptile veterinarian. The correct medications and correct dosages must be used. Because of the small size of the patient, there is no room for error.

External parasites (ectoparasites): Rarely a giant gecko may harbor a tick or two. These are easily removed by daubing the parasite with mineral oil, allowing it to relax for a few minutes,

then carefully removing the creature with tweezers. Be certain that the sucking mouthparts are removed intact. Also be very careful that you do not injure your gecko while restraining it. Some giant geckos have mite pockets on the rear of their thighs. If the gecko is a newly imported specimen, there may be dozens of tiny, red, trombiculid mites present in the pockets. These parasites may also be present wherever a fold of skin exists (neck, tympanum, and legs). A small piece of no pest strip (protected so the lizard cannot come into contact with the chemical-impregnated strip) can be used. Alternatively, the mites can be daubed with a bit of mineral oil and then carefully removed with a dry cotton swab.

Like other geckos, crested geckos eat their shed skins.

Breeding

One of the greatest thrills and challenges for those of us who maintain reptiles is to find and implement the key factors needed to breed the animals successfully. With that said, I hasten to add that our knowledge of the criteria that must be implemented to breed crested and giant geckos is still somewhat rudimentary. Some very successful breeders merely maintain their geckos at room temperature (and this is often quite cool, especially at night), while others artificially manipulate temperature, humidity, and photoperiod, only to fail. One of the largest breeders of crested geckos maintains his gecko room at about 79°F (26°C) year-round and is remarkably successful.

Fortunately, most giant geckos respond well to captive conditions. Once settled in, most will give you many years to manipulate, tweak, then retweak your regimen of husbandry. With luck, you will sooner or later happen on just the right combination of husbandry factors that will induce the lizards to breed. One male may be used to breed with from one to six females.

Using incubators will help you get better hatches.

Note the expanded hemipenial area at the base of the male crested gecko's tail *(right)*.

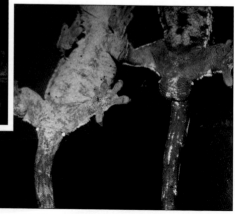

A brightly colored female crested gecko.

A closeup of the eye and snout shape of the crested gecko.

and in midlevel trees, and the giant and the rough-snouted giant geckos are found both in the canopy formed by the tallest trees and at midlevel. The gargoyle gecko is a low-level species, Sarasin's giant gecko occurs in the upper midlevel, and the short-snouted giant gecko at lower midlevel.

Although many of these geckos descend to the ground to nest, some utilize hollow branches for deposition sites. The live-bearing short-snouted giant gecko gives birth in hollow trees.

Natural Habitats

New Caledonia is a southern hemisphere nation that lies east of Australia and north of New Zealand. The coolest temperatures (65–70°F [18–21°C]) occur during the months of June and July (the southern hemisphere winter). The summer months of December through March are the warmest (80–85°F [27–29°C]). Rainfall is the least during the winter and greatest during the summer. Where not destroyed by slash-and-burn farming, logging, or mining, the vegetation is lush and varied. The canopy formed by the tallest trees may be 100 feet (3 km) above the ground. In these forests, the six species of giant gecko are more or less stratified. The crested gecko is found both in shrubs

Criteria Necessary for Breeding

Based on successes so far experienced by breeders of giant geckos and with closely allied geckos of other species, it would seem the criteria needed to breed these creatures should be easy to delineate. However, this is not always so. Certainly providing an adequate diet with ample vitamin and mineral additives and providing suitable caging (including space, temperature, lighting, security, and egg deposition sites) are all important. Of course, unless you have happened to acquire an already gravid adult female, you must also have both sexes of a given species, and these must be compatible. It does seem that giant geckos that are themselves captive bred are easier to cycle than are wild-collected examples. Perhaps that is just because most of the breeding of these interesting geckos is accomplished by hobbyists in the northern hemisphere, where the seasons are exactly the reverse from those where the geckos originate.

Giant geckos may take from a few weeks to a few months to settle into a new cage and to adapt to a new regimen of care. However, once they have become accustomed to their surroundings and staked out their territories, breeding may occur frequently and for many months of the year.

Sex Determination

Females of most species of giant geckos have insignificant preanal pores, while those of the males—especially reproductively active males—are obvious, large, and in several rows. The comparative size of these pores combined with the size of the hemipenial bulges (by far the largest—actually bulbous on adult males) is the best way of determining your gecko's sex.

Egg Basics

All giant geckos deposit soft-shelled eggs, but the eggs of two species have a cursory calcareous overlay. Most captive females bury their clutch of two eggs in the substrate. The soil clings to the damp shells and camouflages the smooth-shelled eggs admirably. Some canopy species prefer to lay their eggs in an elevated situation. These will usually accept a finch-sized nesting box containing 1 to 2 inches (2.5 to 5 cm) of barely moistened soil as the deposition site. The eggs may be single or glued together. If the latter, do not try to separate them. Once the shells have dried, the eggs can be moved to an incubator. The various giant geckos seem to have temperature-dependent sex determination (TDSD), with females being produced at lower temperatures, males at higher temperatures, and both sexes at medium temperatures.

Incubating Gecko Eggs

Suggested incubation temperatures for most of the giant geckos are considerably lower than for other species. A temperature of about 70°F (21°C) seems suitable to produce mostly females of many species, and 78–80°F (26–27°C) produces mostly males. As would be expected, incubation durations are longer for the eggs kept at the lower temperatures. However, the eggs of the crested geckos should be incubated at warmer temperatures. In this species a preponderance of females are produced at an incubation temperature of 79–81°F (26–27°C), while temperatures either slightly above or below these parameters will produce mostly males.

We have successfully used both moistened vermiculite and moistened perlite for incubating mediums. Some breeders prefer using a mixture of the two. Since the soft-shelled eggs of these geckos can desiccate rapidly, it is important to monitor their progress, adding a bit of water to the substrate if the eggs show any indication of losing turgidity. Conversely, it is equally important that the eggs not be over-hydrated. We use an inexact but simple way of determining the proper moisture content of the incubation medium. Moisten the medium thoroughly, then squeeze it as dry as possible in your tightened fists. The eggs should be placed directly onto the substrate in a shallow depression. The exposed top of the eggs can be covered with a paper towel.

Plan to have food of proper size on hand (small crickets and fruit-honey mixture) for when the geckos emerge.

Types of Incubators

An inexpensive incubator (such as a Hovabator) may be purchased commercially from feed and farm supply stores. Be certain that if you choose this avenue, you get an old-style incubator with an adjustable wafer thermostat. The newer models often have a solid-state heating unit that is preset (and unadjustable) to the high temperatures needed to incubate bird's eggs.

Incubators may also be easily made. The needed components are usually available in feed or hardware stores.

Appropriate Conditions

Check the incubator temperature frequently, and add a little water to the incubating medium as needed. The preferred humidity is 80 to 90 percent. A saturated atmosphere, where the moisture condenses and drips onto the eggs is not wanted. The medium of vermiculite or perlite should be damp to the touch but too dry to squeeze out any water when squeezed by your hand. Do not wet the eggs when you are remoistening the medium.

During Incubation

Both infertile and desiccating eggs will collapse during incubation. Infertile eggs usually develop a yellowish, slimy-appearing shell. Discard these. For any number of reasons, embryo death may occur during incubation or even as the full-term young are trying to break from their eggs.

Although it varies by species and temperature, incubation may take between 65 to 88 days. Rarely does incubation last more than 200 days.

Hatching

After pipping, the baby giant geckos (which are often an unrelieved gray in color—crested geckos may be more colorful) may remain in the egg for several hours or may emerge almost immediately. Once they have hatched, they should be moved to another terrarium. Offer food and water after about 48 hours. The hatchlings should have their postnatal shed in from several hours to a few days.

Note the converging crests on the rear of the crested gecko's head.

Making Your Own Incubator

Materials needed for one incubator:

1 wafer thermostat/heater
1 thermometer
1 Styrofoam cooler—one with thick sides (a fish-shipping box is ideal)
1 heat tape or hanging heating coil
1 electrical cord and wall plug
3 wire nuts
1 heavy-wire shelf to hold egg containers 1 to 2 inches (2.5 to 5 cm) above
   the coiled heat tape

Your goal is to wire the wafer thermostat into the circuitry between the heat-transmitting unit and the electrical cord. This will allow you to regulate the temperature of your incubator.

1. Cut the electrical cord (not the heat tape!) about 1 foot (30 cm) from the heat tape. If you use a heating coil, two short electrical leads will be protruding. Do *not* cut these.
2. Poke a hole through the lid of the Styrofoam cooler, and suspend the thermostat/heater from the inside. Add another hole for a thermometer so you can check on the inside temperature without opening the top. If no flange is on the thermometer to keep it from slipping through the hole in the lid, use a rubber band wound several times around the thermometer to form a flange.
3. Poke a hole through the side of the Styrofoam container just large enough to run the electrical wire through.
4. Pull the electrical cord through the side of the incubator.
5. Suspend the heating coil from the top of the incubator, or coil the heat tape loosely on the bottom.
6. Remove about a 1/2 inch (1.3 cm) of insulation from the cut ends of both cords, and separate the wires for about 4 inches (10 cm) back from the cut ends.
7. While carefully following the directions that come with the wafer thermostat and using a wire nut, connect one of the wire leads extending from the heating unit (coil or tape) to the designated red lead extending from the thermostat.
8. Use another wire nut to connect the remaining lead of the thermostat to one of the exposed leads from the wall plug section of the wire.
9. Use the third wire nut to connect the remaining free end of the wall plug section to the remaining unattached lead of the heat tape.

10. Put the lid onto the cooler, and plug in the thermostat/heater.
11. Wait half an hour and check the temperature. Adjust the thermostat/heater by using the L pin (the rheostat) on the top of the thermostat until the temperature inside the incubator attains the temperature you desire.
12. Once you have regulated the temperature, put the egg container holding shelf in place, place the container of eggs onto the shelf inside the incubator, and close the lid.

When handling the eggs, do so carefully after washing your hands. Try to keep the eggs in the position in which they were laid.

A tray of crested gecko eggs with a penny for size comparison.

A day-old crested gecko.

Glossary

Ambient temperature: The temperature of the surrounding environment.

Arboreal: Tree dwelling.

Autotomize: The ability to break easily or voluntarily cast off (and usually to regenerate) a part of the body. This is used with tail breakage in lizards.

Brille: The transparent eye cap or spectacle that covers the eyes of a giant gecko.

Caudal: Pertaining to the tail.

Cloaca: The common chamber into which digestive, urinary, and reproductive systems empty and that itself opens exteriorly through the vent or anus.

Congeners: Species in the same genus.

Deposition: As used here, the laying of the eggs.

Deposition site: The spot chosen by the female to lay her eggs.

Dorsal: Pertaining to the back; upper surface.

Dorsolateral: Pertaining to the upper sides.

Dorsum: The upper surface.

Gravid: The reptilian equivalent of mammalian pregnancy.

Juvenile: A young or immature specimen.

Lamellae: The transverse scales that extend across the underside of a giant gecko's toes and tail tip.

Lateral: Pertaining to the side.

Middorsal: Pertaining to the middle of the back.

Midventral: Pertaining to the center of the belly or abdomen.

Ontogenetic: Age-related changes.

Oviparous: Reproducing by means of eggs that hatch after laying.

Posterior: Toward the rear.

Scansor: *See* lamellae.

Subdigital: Beneath the toes.

Taxon: A species (*taxa* is the plural).

Thermoregulate: To regulate (body) temperature by choosing a warmer or cooler environment.

Vent: The external opening of the cloaca; the anus.

Venter: The underside of a creature; the belly.

Ventral: Pertaining to the undersurface or belly.

Ventrolateral: Pertaining to the sides of the venter; the belly.

Other scientific definitions are contained in the following two volumes:

Peters, James A. 1964. *Dictionary of Herpetology.* New York: Hafner Publishing Co.

Wareham, David C. 1993. *The Reptile and Amphibian Keeper's Dictionary.* London: Blandford.

Helpful Information

Herpetological Societies

Reptile and amphibian groups exist in the form of clubs, monthly magazines, professional societies, and online chat rooms in addition to the herp expos and other commercial functions mentioned elsewhere.

Herpetological societies (or clubs) exist in major cities in North America, Europe, and other areas of the world. Most have monthly meetings; some publish newsletters; many host or sponsor field trips and picnics or indulge in various other interactive functions. Among the members are enthusiasts of varying expertise. Information about these clubs can often be learned by querying pet shop employees, high school science teachers, university biology professors, or curators or employees at the Department of Herpetology at local museums and zoos. All such clubs welcome inquiries and new members.

Two of the professional herpetological societies are

Society for the Study of Amphibians
    and Reptiles (SSAR)
Yale University
New Haven, CT 06520

Herpetologist's League
Division of Biological Sciences
Emporia State University
Emporia, KS 66801

The SSAR publishes two quarterly journals: *Herpetological Review* contains husbandry, range extensions, news on ongoing field studies, and so on, while the *Journal of Herpetology* contains articles oriented more toward academic herpetology.

One hobbyist magazine that publishes articles on all aspects of herpetology and herpetoculture (including lizards) is

Reptiles
P.O. Box 6050
Mission Viejo, CA 92690

Hobbyist magazines also carry classified ads and news about herp expos.

The classified ads on *www.kingsnake.com* are a wonderful resource for geckos and other herps, and *PetPlace.com* is a good source of general information about many species.

Kingsnake.com is an important web site. It provides both classified ads and gecko forums. Avail yourself of this resource.

Index

Page numbers set in boldface type indicate photographs.

The back of the crested gecko is often some shade of tan.